PDX BY BIKE

Your guide to discovering Portland, Oregon by bicycle.

by Meghan Sinnott and Elly Blue

illustrated by Matt Gauck
designed by Joe Biel & Elly Blue
fonts by Ian Lynam

Second edition, January 2012

The print companion to *PDXbyBike.com*

This zine is dedicated to all of our friends, mentors, and colleagues who have written about bicycling in Portland. You inspire us!

Table of Contents

Introduction

Hello! We're Meghan and Elly. Between us we have over 15 years experience riding around Portland and organizing bicycle events. We love exploring our city's vast variety of bike rides and bike oriented businesses.

We started PDX by Bike in Meghan's living room with the goal of helping you discover the city we love on your own two wheels.

We've put together everything we know about bicycling in Portland, boiled it down to the basics, and presented it here for you to plan your escapades, and to keep in your pocket as you explore.

We hope our observations help you feel at home while bicycling in Portland. Maybe you already live here and are just getting started bicycling, or perhaps you are just here for the weekend. Either way, we want you to feel confident hopping on a bike to go wherever you want, and knowing that you are doing it with style and grace. Or... at least that you are doing it like a local.

This zine* is a companion to *PDXbyBike.com*, where we offer specific information about where to stay, how to get here, and what to do. Our promise is to give you the best information available about bicycling in Portland. We invite you to drop us a line at *info@pdxbybike.com* to suggest additions and corrections, buy a custom itinerary, or just to say hello.

Sincerely,

Meghan and Elly

* *zine* is an abbreviation for "fanzine," a small, self-published booklet about a specific area of interest, compiled with a devotion that borders on obsession.

Getting Around Portland

A bike map will help you immensely with finding the best routes. Meghan prefers Metro's beautiful, tear-proof, water-resistant bike maps of the region—we sell them at *shop.pdxbybike.com.* Elly's budget tip is to pick up the city's free, pocket-sized bike map. You can request one at *gettingaroundportland.org*

Orientation

Portland is separated into five "quadrants:" NW, SW, NE, SE, and N. The Willamette River divides the city into its east and west sides, while Burnside Street separates the north from the south. North Portland is a wedge on the east side of the Willamette, separated from Northeast by N Williams Ave. Most streets on which you travel north and south are numbered (like 5th Ave). Think of the river as zero; numbers go up as you head either east or west. In Northwest, most of the named streets are alphabetical (Burnside, Couch, Davis, etc.). A few alphabetical streets appear in Northeast, too.

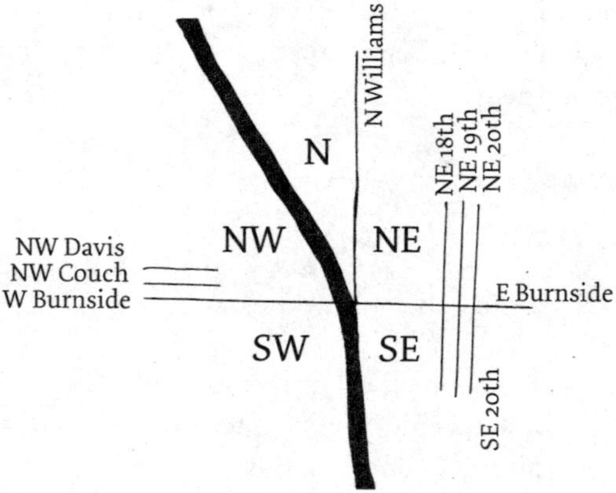

Bike the Bridges!

There are many bridges across the Willamette, and some are far more bicycle-friendly than others. Below are your best bets. Be sure to read our tips for shared path etiquette on page 7.

Steel Bridge

Hawthorne A wide, shared sidewalk that is very congested during rush hour. Always ride in the same direction as car traffic. Shared path etiquette is extra important here.

Burnside Other than the actual bridge crossing (wide bike lanes on the same grade as car traffic), riding on Burnside itself isn't anyone's idea of fun. On the east side, the Ankeny bike boulevard (one block south of Burnside) is your best approach. Couch, one block north, is a good westbound option if you're confident handling faster traffic and the infamous right hook intersection at MLK. E Burnside itself has a new bike lane from the bridge up to 13th Ave, but it isn't very enjoyable. On the west side, take Couch. Coming west off the bridge, turn right first chance you get. If you're going east, turn left onto Burnside from NW 3rd Ave.

Morrison Not our favorite bridge. The wide, new path on the south side of the bridge is meant for walking and biking in both directions. On the east end, you'll be crossing a blind freeway exit and then potentially getting stuck for half an hour in the rain waiting for a train to pass. On the west end, it's a confusing mess.

Steel The lower deck boasts a carfree, though narrow, path that is obvious and accessible from the Eastbank Esplanade (that's the beautiful biking and walking path along the river's east side) and Waterfront Park (its sister path to the west). Check out your map for access from the street. We don't recommend trying to bike across the top of this bridge, though it's technically possible, and too easy to do accidentally on the west end.

Broadway A wide sidewalk, shared with pedestrian traffic. Ride only in the same direction as traffic. Heading west off of the bridge, there is a bike-only signal to get you safely into downtown.

I-5 Bridge Sometimes you might want to cross the Columbia, too! You can bike on the sidewalk of the I-5 bridge into Vancouver, Washington. It feels death-defying, but it's totally doable. The hardest part is finding your way to the bridge on the Oregon side. The Portland/Vancouver bike map makes it a lot easier—you can get one from *gettingaroundportland.org*

Mount Tabor Okay, this isn't a bridge, and it isn't even a real mountain, but you still need to know how to get over—or rather, around—this close-in butte. Tabor affects your route east of about SE 50th and west of SE 82nd between SE Division and E Burnside. The bike maps make SE Lincoln seem like the best route, but you'll save time and keep yourself from getting turned around if you just ride up NE Davis to the north or SE Woodward to the south. On the other hand, if you're not in a hurry, enjoy getting a little lost, and are looking for a picnic spot with some good views of Portland, then head straight for the top!

How to Ride a Bike in Portland

Biking in Portland is easy and intuitive—for the most part. Like any city, we have our own peculiar laws and norms. You'll maximize your enjoyment if you keep a few tips in mind to avoid run-ins on the road and with the law. Portland police aggressively enforce bicycle traffic laws, not only in the downtown core but also on quiet back streets when there is nobody else around.

Here are our tips for riding in Portland. **Legal requirements are in bold**. Everything else is advisable—use your judgment and common sense!

Don't be a salmon! **Ride your bike in the same direction that you would drive a car.**

Stop on red. **Stop at stop signs and wait at red lights** or be prepared for a $242 ticket. You do have to stop, but you do not need to put your foot down.

Lighten up. At night and on really rainy days, **you need a white front light and a red rear reflector or light.** We recommend always taking your lights in with you when you leave your bike parked outside.

Stay away from parked cars. Give them a wide berth and don't weave in and out when there are gaps.

Take the lane. You are legally allowed to take the car lane **if you are preparing to turn left, if there is no bike lane or shoulder, or if you are avoiding a hazard**—like the door zone, glass or gravel, a pothole, or a double parked car. It's often a good idea.

> Ride with confidence!
> *- Meghan Sinnott, co-author*

Signal your turns. **Use your arms to signal left and right turns**. You're supposed to signal your stops, too, but nobody does this. If you do not feel it is safe to take your hands off the handle bars, you don't have to.

Yield to pedestrians. If you are able to stop safely, **you must let people walk across the street at any intersection** if they look like they want to cross, even if there isn't a striped crosswalk.

Stay off the sidewalk. You may legally ride on the sidewalk anywhere except in downtown Portland. That doesn't mean it's a good idea. If you must, yield to people walking, give an audible warning when you pass, and ride at walking speed at driveways and intersections.

Make some noise! **You must audibly signal your intention to pass.** If you are passing another biker or a pedestrian, please ring your bell or say "on your left." Either way, give plenty of advance warning.

Passing cars. We don't recommend lane-splitting unless traffic is at an absolute standstill. But in Oregon, **you are legally allowed to pass car traffic on the right if it is safe to do so.** Always be cautious when doing this—never pass in an intersection! Yield to cars that might be turning. Sadly, you can't always expect them to signal.

right turn!

Beware the hook. Stay sharp at intersections. People in cars (or on bikes!) turning left or right across your path may not see you or signal.

Ride well with others. Visitors to our city often find that they need to adjust their riding style in order to deal with our heavy traffic—bicycle traffic, that is.

left turn!

Passing bikes. Pass other bicyclists on the left, never on the right. They don't expect you there. Also, we spit to the right. Never pass in the bike lane, it's too much of a squeeze—merge safely to the next lane over first.

Share the path. Portland's many paved, multi-use paths are free of cars and full of beauty—but have a surprisingly high crash rate. Only pass on the left. If you're going slow, bike far enough to the right so faster bikers can pass you. Always be aware on paths, slow down when anybody else is around, give walkers (especially ones with dogs and children) plenty of leeway. **Never ride the wrong way over the bridges.** Watch out for speed demons, close passers, wrong way riders, meandering children, groups of joggers, and dogs.

Yield! **You must yield to anyone in front of you.** It doesn't matter what mode they're using or what shenanigans they're up to. Assume that anyone ahead of you will swerve or stop suddenly, and plan for it.

Helmet up... it's the law **until you're 16.** Across the Columbia River, in Vancouver, Washington, everyone must wear a helmet.

Mind the tracks. Watch out for MAX, streetcar and train tracks! They will eat your tire, and are slippery

> Watch out for streetcar tracks.
> *–Chris Balduc, Deaf Power Organization*

when wet. Cross them at a steady speed and a 90° angle, without turning. Don't let the cars behind you rush you into making poor decisions. They can wait.

Choose your route. Pay attention to the colored lines on the bike map. If you like to ride slow, go for the quieter back streets over busy ones with bike lanes. If you like riding fast, choose faster streets. Whatever you do, avoid major arterials like MLK, Powell, and SE 39th Ave.

Slippery stuff. Watch out for these things when it's wet out: leaves, metal plates, manhole covers, the green bike lanes and boxes, rail tracks, and the fake bricks the city loves to put downtown.

U-lock is for locking. Don't ride around with an "I've got my U-lock in my hand" mentality. Many drivers in Portland bike too. Don't assume it's "us against them."

Speaking of u-locks... You're going to have to park your bike at some point. Avoid getting it stolen by always using a u-lock (cable locks can be cut like butter). Be sure to lock the frame to something sturdy, and try to lock at least one wheel, too. Don't lock to handrails or trees, or the officials will be the ones making off with your bike.

run the u-lock through a wheel and the parking staple

Fancy Infrastructure Guide

Bike routes. You can ride on any road, but some of them are a lot more fun than others. Study your map before setting out. Along your way, keep an eye out for bike wayfinding signs that point you to your destination; also watch out for bike lanes that end suddenly, and be prepared to get creative.

Bike box! When the light is green, ignore the bike box. When the light is red, use it to get a jump on car traffic and slower bike traffic, avoiding both exhaust fumes and the dreaded right hook. Look out for drivers who might not use them properly.

Green lanes. In high-conflict areas, bike lanes are entirely covered in green thermoplastic. Be extra cautious. Think of these markings as a reminder that drivers do stupid things in these areas--not that they are extra safe due to some extra paint.

Left-turn boxes. You'll occasionally come across a left turn box on a street where conditions make it impossible to merge left before you turn. Continue straight through the intersection, stopping in the green box. Then turn your bike 90 degrees to the left and continue forward when that light turns green.

a bike box

the common sharrow

Sharrows. The word "sharrow" is an amalgamation of "share the road" and "arrows." You'll find many low-traffic streets criss-crossing Portland painted with giant bicycles topped by chevrons that point the way forward. Sharrows don't have any legal meaning. They just indicate a heavily traveled bike route and also show you where to ride in the road and the direction in which you'll find good major street crossings and fewer stop signs.

Bike lanes. The most prosaic of all bike infrastructure, bike lanes still require special care. Ride with confidence, but be wary of opening car doors, of drivers turning right, and of people parking or stepping out between parked cars. Don't be afraid to leave the lane if it's filled with gravel or glass—just be sure to check over your shoulder before you do. And, as with all street markings, please be careful when crossing lines in the rain, as they may slippery!

Regular travel lanes. Despite popular belief, these are not just for cars. When in doubt, take the lane, riding at least four feet from the right. This will help you avoid getting hit by a car door and signal to drivers behind you that they must cross to the next lane to pass. Never weave in and out between parked cars while hugging the right—this is unpredictable and scary for drivers. If you want to let someone pass you, wait until it's safe and then merge to the right. Most drivers you encounter will be relatively polite—even when they get frustrated, they don't tend to get violent.

> Incorporate neighborhood riding as much as possible.
>
> *– Dave Guettler, owner of River City Bicycles*

Riding downtown. Always take the lane in downtown Portland. The traffic lights are timed to 12-15mph, so nobody in a car will be able to get anywhere faster than you can, no matter how much they'd like to. Ride in the middle of whichever lane you feel most comfortable in. Make sure you don't use the bus and rail lanes on the transit mall, and never ride in the same lane as rail tracks. If there's a lot of traffic, it can sometimes be faster to walk a few blocks.

The bike stripe. Some stop lights don't automatically turn green unless they detect a car waiting at the intersection. Fortunately, if you position your bike correctly, it can also trigger most of these car sensors. The little white line on the road with a bike icon in the center is your guide.

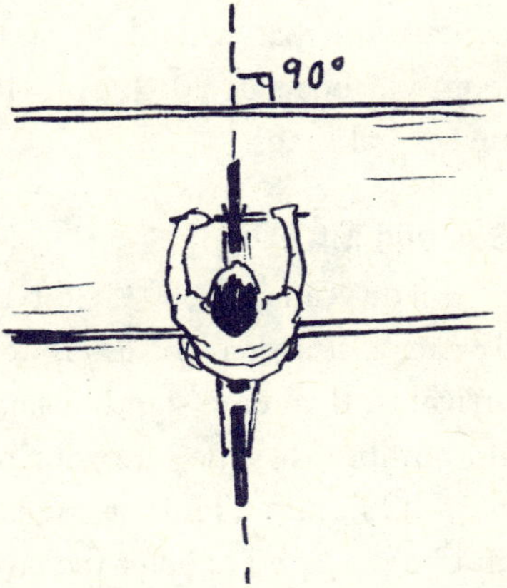

cross rail tracks at as close as possible to a 90 degree angle

Take Transit!

every bus has a bike rack on the front

Portland's transit system boasts good bus coverage, with many lines promising "frequent service" every 17 minutes or less. The light rail system (called the MAX) takes you through downtown and to the airport and several suburbs. We also have an ever-expanding streetcar system that boasts stops every few blocks along its routes in the center city.

It is FREE to take your bike with you on all forms of transit in Portland.

Heads up!

As of press time, MAX and Streetcar are free downtown; that will likely end. The eastside Streetcar loop will open in 2012. And fares will undoubtably go up several times.

Bus and MAX

You can call 503.238.RIDE or use the Transit Tracker feature on *TriMet.org* to find out when the next arrival is. If you are standing at a stop, look for the "Stop ID number" to type into your phone. If you can't find a Stop ID number, look for the largest intersection nearby and be prepared to enter the cross streets when you call.

For advance planning, the online trip planner on the home page of *TriMet.org* is invaluable. They've also just launched a cutting-edge trip planning feature that combines transit and bicycling, at *rtp.TriMet.org.* It's still in beta, so take its directions with a grain of salt.

The least you can pay for a ticket is $2.10. (Unless you're over 65, then a ride will only cost a buck!) This will get you unlimited rides in any direction on any line within two "zones" for about two hours. Unless you're going really far (like to the end of the line), you'll probably be staying within a two-zone area.

The base fare for anything farther than 2 zones is $2.40. All-zone tickets can be used on C-TRAN (the bus system in Vancouver, Washington) as well.

Pay with exact change when you board a bus, or use a card or cash to buy tickets at MAX stations, or get multiple tickets in advance at Fred Meyer stores or the kiosk behind the waterfall in Pioneer Square—you'll need to validate these right before getting on the MAX. Your ticket is your transfer. Keep it until it expires.

If you plan on riding transit at least three times in one day with your trips spaced more than an hour or two apart, it might be worth your money to get the day pass for $5. Or you can buy a 7 day pass, but it's only a good deal if you plan to make more than two trips per day.

Each bus has a rack on the front with two slots. If they're both full, which happens often, you'll need to wait for the next bus or have a backup plan. Useful videos can be found online at *pdx.be/buseslovebikes*

> Biking is usually faster than TriMet.
>
> *– Gabriel Amadeus, graphic designer*

Meghan's tips for getting your bike on the bus

Putting your bike on the bus for the first time is daunting, and it's safe to assume nobody will help you. Take the front space if it's available. Really pay attention to which tire is supposed to go in which slot. Pull the bar as far up over your front tire as possible. I have seen it slip off wet wheels before. Don't be afraid to get a little rough with the rack. You won't hurt it. (Though be warned, it does slam down pretty hard if you don't ease it open.) Don't forget to tell the driver that you're retrieving your bike when you exit the bus!

MAX (light rail)

The MAX light rail is run by TriMet, same as the bus. Buy your ticket before you board. You can use a credit card or cash at the machines. Your ticket for the MAX is also your transfer and works on the bus—and vise versa. Transit police come through and check for tickets regularly.

bike parking on the MAX

Meghan's tips for putting your bike on the MAX

When I put my bike up, I give the seat a boost with my right hip. My arms aren't as strong as I'd like them to be. Also, sit so you can see your bike as you ride. Bikes are sometimes stolen from the MAX.

The streetcar and the tram

Portland's streetcar system is run by a private company, not by TriMet, but your bus or MAX ticket will still work as a transfer. As of press time, the streetcar is free in the downtown core, but there are plans to start collecting fares in 2012. Streetcar fares have never been enforced regularly, but that may change as the system expands to the inner east side.

The streetcar is slow! If you walk, you can keep up with it or even outpace it. That doesn't mean it isn't a pleasant ride, but if you get there and the next train comes in 20 minutes, it usually isn't worth waiting.

We don't recommend trying to take the streetcar on a gorgeous day. It will be packed and you'll have more fun getting where you're going by bike.

The streetcar (or your bike) can take you directly to the South Waterfront district and the aerial tram that scales the West Hills with spectacular views. The tram costs $4 to ride up and is free to go back down. You can bring your bike on it. There's nothing at the top but the hospital, so the view is the only reason you'd want to go.

Riding a long distance like 10+ miles isn't hard at all and is faster than you think. Just the hills are a bitch.

– Siobhan Doyle, graphic designer

Group Ride Guide

Here are some tips for riding in GROUPS. Whether you're planning on a group ride marathon during Pedalpalooza or you've ventured out with a Midnight Mystery Ride, here's what to know:

- Don't swerve around or stop suddenly in front of (tall) bike riders.
- If you don't know where the ride is going, stick to the back.
- Make your lights solid rather than blinky so you don't give anyone a seizure. Turn them off at the end location.
- If the light turns red and there are people "corking" the street (i.e. blocking traffic with the green light), then you should just proceed through the intersection if safe to do so. (This is not legal advice!)
- If you are at the front of the ride and come to a red light, yell "stopping!" and stop.
- Don't follow anyone too closely.
- Try not to pass on the right.
- Let people know you're passing them. You can bing yer bell, but it's even better to say "on your left!"
- Inform the ride leader if people are straggling behind due to red lights or flat tires.
- At the end of the ride, you'll find people happy to give you directions or even ride with you back to a familiar part of town.

How to Yell in Portland

On group rides, communication is key.

- Yell "clear!" if there is nobody coming at you in an intersection.
- Yell "car!" if there is a car coming and bikers are still following behind you through an intersection.
- Yell "car up!" if there is a car coming towards you and there are people clearly in its path.
- Yell "car back" if there is an aggressive driver behind the ride trying to pass.
- Yell "bus!" if there is a bus trying to do its thing. Never interfere with TriMet!
- Yell "pepper!" if you see a cop and people aren't doing what they're supposed to be doing.
- Yell "pole!" if you pass by pole in the middle of a path.
- Yell "pothole!" if you narrowly miss a nasty pothole.
- Yell "glass!" or "tacks!" if there are sharp things in the street.

> Follow the arrows on the ground, like a video game.
>
> *– Matt Gauck, drawist*

> Best way to party hop, EVER.
>
> *– Gabriel Amadeus, ambassador of bike fun*

Rides and Events To Remember

Portland boasts countless bike events each year. This list is just a sampling. See *PDXbyBike.com* for more events and exact dates and places.

Once a year

January

New Year's Day Ride – A fifty-five year long tradition, now led by the Bicycle Transportation Alliance. Rain, sleet, or shine!

Palm Tree Ride – Your chance to explore Portland's little known tropical landscape.

February

Mini Bike Winter – Three awesome days of bike tomfoolery, including the Ben Hurt chariot wars and the aerial-aquatic Cupcake Challenge. If you're new to Portland-style bike shenanigans, look for a few videos online to get yourself acquainted first. You don't have to have a freak bike or a kid's bike to join in on the fun. Costumes and cheap drinks recommended.

April

Filmed by Bike – An independent, multi day film fest of short bike movies from all over the world. The Friday night opening street party is not to be missed.

Bunny on a Bike Ride – A mellow, costumed family ride on Easter Sunday.

Pedal Nation Bike Show – A big trade show with exhibits and events highlighting diverse aspects of the local bike industry.

June

Pedalpalooza – 2+ weeks of bike fun every June. Get a copy of the calendar in the Mercury or find it online at *shift2bikes.org* There are hundreds of totally free events that anyone can join.

Multnomah County Bike Fair – MCBF wraps up Pedalpalooza. Come for the spectacle and tall bike bike jousting, stay for the activities, exhibitions, and booths. Good fun for all ages.

World Naked Bike Ride - The WNBR isn't unique to Portland, we just do it best with record numbers. It happens in June during Pedalpalooza. Thousands of bikers gather and get "as bare as they dare" and then tool around town. People of all shapes, sizes, genders, ages and biking skill levels are welcome.

Daytime Naked Ride – A smaller, more activist naked ride, for those who prefer to make a statement without the alcohol, the party crowd, and the police escort.

Cirque du Cycling – A family fun festival featuring a bustling street fair, a freakbike parade, and an on-street criterium race.

July

Seattle to Portland (STP) – A beautiful 200+ mile ride that you can do in one or two days, with convivial camping in the middle. Benefits bike advocacy in Washington (the state).

August

Bridge Pedal – 20,000 people ride over bridges and on the freeway. In between stunning bridge views, you can relish the rare experience of true bicycle traffic gridlock. This one's not free.

Twilight Criterium – Professional bike racing in downtown Portland.

September

Oregon Manifest – Bicycle constructors innovate and build bikes intended for everyday urban riding—and then race them.

October

Cross Crusade – Waffles, coffee, mud, and bike racing. Fun to watch, and extraordinarily accessible to race. Kids and dogs each have their own course.

Oregon Handmade Bicycle Show - The art and craft of bicycle framebuilding on awe-inspiring display.

December

BikeCraft – Dozens of local producers of handmade goods converge at this craft fair to sell everything from bike-themed t-shirts to crocheted top tube cozies to bike-inspired art. It's a great place to hang out and meet bike people out of the winter weather.

You can show up and feel welcome at any bike event.

– Meghan Sinnott, co-author

All summer

Sunday Parkways – several per year. Eight miles of residential streets go carfree and tens of thousands of people ride from park to park, smiling ear to ear and stopping frequently for ice cream and activities.

Munday Funday – every week. Dodgeball, kickball, and low key hanging out. On sunny days someone often brings a bike sound system. No bike required.

Kidical Mass – sporadic. What's cuter than a dozen families riding through the streets, stopping at all the stop signs, dinging their bells, and then getting ice cream?

Every month

Midnight Mystery Ride (MMR) – second Fridays. It begins at a bar and leaves at midnight for a usually outdoor destination. All are welcome. Find the blog to get the start location after noon on the day of the ride. Bring your map and enough beverages to last you through the night.

Breakfast on the Bridges – last Friday of every month and every Friday in June. Free coffee, donuts, and camaraderie from 7-9am on the Hawthorne (and sometimes Steel) bridge.

Bicycle Brown Bag – third Thursdays, noon - 1pm. A free public talk about colorful topics ranging from bike infrastructure in the Netherlands to bike touring in Oregon.

Vegan Dinner Ride – first Fridays. Ride to a vegan restaurant and maybe later to a bar with vegan drinks.

Dropout Ride – third Fridays. A spirited parade of tall bikes, choppers, freak bikes, mini bikes, and regular bicycles that rides deep into the night, accompanied by bicycle-mounted sound systems.

Critical Mass – This doesn't happen much in Portland anymore.

Werewolf Hustle – Every full moon, 8pm sharp. Meet at the food carts at SE 12th & Hawthorne to ride 15 to 20 mph for 15 to 30 miles.

Every week

Zoobomb – every Sunday night. Don't call the police when you hear someone exclaim, "We're going bombing!" In this case, "bomb" means to ride down a big hill fast. Zoobombing entails taking the MAX to the Zoo exit and cruising back into town en masse, usually on kids' bikes. If you are interested in joining in, we recommend you read the *New to Zoobomb* page at zoobomb.net. Meet seasoned Zoobombers at 8:30pm at the Pyle (an unmistakeable sculpture at SW 13th and W Burnside), borrow a mini-bike, and follow them to the MAX and up the hill.

Bike Polo – Several times a week, but Sunday afternoons at Alberta Park are your best bet. A fun sport to watch, and if you're inspired to join in there's usually a loaner bike and mallet and someone friendly to show you the ropes.

Lingo to Know

Bike Corrals. On-street parking spots that have been retrofitted to fit ten or twenty bikes. The concept of the corrals was greeted with initial skepticism, but since the first six were installed the city has not been able to keep up with the demand.

BikePortland. "Did you see that thing on BikePortland?" is surely something you'll overhear walking past a crowded coffeeshop. Jonathan Maus' Bikeportland.org is where bikers all over go for up-to-date information on bike related news, businesses, trends, and events.

Corking. Corking is when cyclists block cross-traffic at intersections so that a group can stay together and not get separated. It's not legal, but it is helpful for very large rides.

Couch. Couch is a street, not a sofa. Pronounce it "cootch." Seriously, this isn't just some joke we play on newbies.

The Couv. Vancouver, Washington. Not to be confused with the more metropolitan Canadian city.

Freak Bike. A tall bike, art bike or freak bike can all refer to a bike made of two or more frames stacked and welded together. Only outsiders call them "art bikes," though. And there are more than just tall freak bikes. Choppers, gravity bikes, and swing bikes are just a few other examples. There are many freak bike clubs, groups, and gangs in town.

> When in Rome...
>
> *– Shawn Granton, Urban Adventure League*

CHUNK 666, the oldest, has largely dropped below the radar. Others include Dropout Bicycle Club (DOBC or just Dropout), North Freak, and the Dead Babies.

The Merc(ury). A free weekly newspaper. Check for the new one every Thursday. It has a well-curated page of events and thorough movie and music listings.

Move by Bike. MxB is one of the best happenings in Portland! Want to meet some locals and experience something wacky? Lend a hand on a bike move. People post their plans on the Shift calendar and strangers show up with bikes and bike trailers and haul their belongings across town in a big parade, for free!

Oregon. It's "ORE-uh-gun." Not "ori-GONE."

pod. A cluster of food carts, often sharing an ATM and a central, covered eating area.

The River. Pronounce it "wuh-LAM-it."

Shift. Shift is a group of dedicated bike funnists who love organizing free, grassroots, often whimsical events. Shift puts on Pedalpalooza, bike moves, Breakfast on the Bridges (BonB), and hundreds of other fun happenings throughout the year. You can find a calendar and discussion listserv at shift2bikes.org.

Sprockettes. An all-ladies synchronized mini-bike dance troupe. If you see a woman clad in black and hot pink, riding a tiny bike, you're probably looking at a Sprockette.

don't get doored! ride at least four feet from parked cars

The Back Story on the Bike Story

For your amusement and edification, here are some scenes from Portland's bike history:

- During the Golden Age of Bicycling, between 1885 and 1905, businessman Fred T. Merril sold 52,000 bicycles in Portland. Then he switched to selling cars.
- In 1896, the city's first bicycle path was built, paid for by local members of the Wheelmen club who wanted a paved route to their favorite bar.
- In 1971, Oregon passed the Bicycle Bill, requiring that bike and walking facilities be included on all new or rebuilt state-funded roads. Essentially, what this means is for every $1 spent on roads, about 1¢ goes to improvements for non-motorized road users. This only began to be enforced in 1995 when the Bicycle Transportation Alliance won a lawsuit forcing the city to build bike lanes through the Rose Quarter.
- On the last Friday of September in 1993 over 100 people took part in Portland's first Critical Mass. The tradition had begun the year before in San Francisco and was soon to take off worldwide. In 1995, 17 participants won over $50,000 in a First Amendment lawsuit against the city of Portland after many of them were arrested in Pioneer Square. By 2008, the controversial monthly rides had all but ended.
- In 2002, Portland hosted Bike Summer, a month of grassroots bicycle rides and events from the silly to the sporty. That summer's legacy continues in our annual Pedalpalooza, two and a half weeks of bike fun capped by the riotous, family friendly Multnomah County Bike Fair.

• By 2008, Portland had a 274 mile bikeway network. The total cost of this infrastructure was about the same as a single mile of urban freeway: $65 million.

• Portland has the largest World Naked Bike Ride in the world. In 2009 there were a record-setting 5,000 naked riders, with even more participants in 2010, though counts vary widely.

> Have more bike fun!
>
> *– Shift's unofficial motto*

Elly's tips for increasing your bike nerd power

If you've been wondering why bikes are such a big deal all of a sudden, pick up a copy of Portland journalist Jeff Mapes' book *Pedaling Revolution: How Cyclists are Changing American Cities*. It's a history of the bicycle transportation movement in the United States, including an excellent chapter on Portland.

If you live here in town, check out the Traffic & Transportation class at Portland State University's school of planning. It's a weekly evening class taught by a team of knowledgable movers and shakers. Free, non-credit spots are available every year for community members who want to learn to be transportation activists. The class is an amazing resource and has led many an everyday Portlander to be overheard bandying about terms like "mode split" and "MUTCD."

Where to Use the internet

We want you to have easy access to up-to-date information. With your own laptop, you can use free wireless internet just about anywhere that you can get a cup of coffee. There are some surprising exceptions, so be sure to ask before ordering. There are also still a few places around town with computers you can use:

- *Multnomah County Library* 503.988.5123 There are library branches all over town and each has multiple computers for you to surf the web. Out of town visitors can get a computer guest pass by showing a valid photo ID. Usage limited to one hour per day total, even if you switch locations. Ask around or call to find a branch.
- *Umpqua Bank* Many locations around the city, including 1139 NW Lovejoy, 7851 SE 13th, 1745 NE Alberta, and 3557 SE Hawthorne. Multiple computers are available to the public for free during banking hours, so long as you don't mind being prominently on display in their plate glass windows while you check your email. 30 minute limit, or ask.
- *Smith Memorial Student Union* at Portland State University, 1825 SW Broadway. Two web kiosks are available on each of the first two floors. Intended for quick use.
- *Backspace* 115 NW 5th Ave. The only full-on internet café remaining in Portland, catering mainly to gamers. $6 an hour, with a minimum of $3. If you pay the $30 yearly membership fee, you get a free day after which it's only $3 an hour. Open from 7am on weekdays and 10am on weekends until midnight.
- *Grendel's Coffee House* 727 E Burnside. Two (kinda clunky) computers available for customers. When it's busy, they ask you to limit your use to 20 minutes.

Essential Resources

PDXbyBike.com for more tips on getting around by bike, places to stay, bike rentals, and more

GettingAroundPortland.org for bike maps, route advisories, and more information from the city

PortlandMercury.com for news, arts, music, and movie times

Bikeportland.org for local transportation-related news, views, events, and culture

Shift2bikes.org for bike fun, resources, and rides

RideOregonRide.com for discovering our state's great outdoors by bike

And finally, a wealth of legal and safety advice from our friends at **stc-law.com/bikelinks.html**

Numbers to know

- Emergency: 911
- Police non-emergency: 503.823.3333
- Report hazards in the bike lane: 503.823.BUMP
- Bus schedules: 503.238.7433
- Taxi: 503.227.1212
- Bike rentals: 503.227.1719

Ten digit dialing!

When making a phone call within Portland you must dial the area code (usually 503, some newer cell phones are 971) before the seven-digit phone number. When making calls outside of the Portland area, you need to dial a 1 first. Strangely, a few 503 numbers outside of the Portland area—in Salem, for instance—do require you to dial a 1.

About the Authors

Meghan Sinnott plans bicycle events by night and works as a social worker by day, helping keep low-income people housed. Meghan's trusty steed is an white 80s Bianchi with an absurdly large front basket. On this bike she leads Midnight Mystery Rides, joins freakbike rides, hauls sound systems, tasty beverages, and freebox finds. She rides everywhere.

Elly Blue writes about bicycle transportation. Her work has appeared in Grist, Bitch, BikePortland, Momentum, Reclaim, and on her own blog and print zine, both called Taking the Lane. When she isn't writing, she can be spotted riding around Portland on her longtail bike, often carrying her boyfriend on a six foot bamboo trailer.

PDX by Bike is our way to help you make the most of bicycling in Portland. We're like bike concierges. Or matchmakers. Portland's bike scene truly has something for everyone, and we'd love to connect you with the experiences that spark your inner biker flame.

Feeling overwhelmed? Get in touch! We're excited to help you have a great time visiting and bicycling in our city. Our website has up-to-date information that anyone can use, and we also offer custom itineraries that empower you to discover Portland on your own two wheels.

Email us: info@PDXbyBike.com
Like us: facebook.com/PDXbyBike
Follow us: twitter.com/PDXbyBike

NOTES